D0719403

The First Andrew W. Mellon Lecture

January 23, 1976

GEORGETOWN UNIVERSITY

GEORGETOWN UNIVERSITY PRESS

WASHINGTON, D.C.

1. 9. 21

Library of Congress Cataloging in Publication Data

Di Pietro, Robert J
    Language as human creation.

    (The Andrew W. Mellon lecture ;   1976)
    Bibliography
    1.   Creative ability (Linguistics)   2.   Languages—
Psychology.   I.   Title.   II.   Series.
P37.D5   401   76-25157
ISBN 0-87840-166-0

Copyright © 1976 by Georgetown University Press,
Washington, D.C.   20007   All rights reserved

PRINTED IN THE UNITED STATES OF AMERICA
INTERNATIONAL STANDARD BOOK NUMBER: 0-87840-166-0

GEORGETOWN UNIVERSITY

School of Languages and Linguistics
The Andrew W. Mellon Fund
Distinguished Lectureship
in Languages and Linguistics

This is an honorary title, established under a grant from the Andrew W. Mellon Foundation of New York for a permanent endowment for support of the academic activities of the School of Languages and Linguistics. Within this grant, the Andrew W. Mellon Fund Distinguished Lectureship in languages and linguistics was created. This Lectureship was established to recognize distinguished professors who are outstanding in the field of linguistics, who have a broad interest in linguistics, language and culture, and whose approaches are humanistic in character.

Robert J. Di Pietro, Ph.D.
1975-76   1976-77

Introduction

James E. Alatis, *Dean*

Georgetown University
School of Languages and Linguistics

<small>Distinguished Members of the Faculty,
Ladies, and Gentlemen:</small>

It is with great pleasure that I announce this evening the establishment of the Andrew W. Mellon Fund Distinguished Lectureship in Languages and Linguistics, which honors those faculty members of the Georgetown University School of Languages and Linguistics who have made outstanding contributions to the field of the language sciences, both through their scholarship and through their teaching. This honorary title, bestowed once every two years and which includes a small stipend, pays tribute to the broad interests in linguistics, language, and culture associated with those professors whose approaches are especially humanistic in character.

This evening, we honor the first recipient of this award. After consultation with the Faculty of the School of Languages and Linguistics, it is my pleasure to announce that Professor Robert J. Di Pietro of the Department of Linguistics has been chosen as the Andrew W. Mellon Distinguished Lecturer for the academic years 1975–1976 and 1976–1977.

Linguistics, standing at the crossroads of many disciplines, offers an opportunity for the pursuit of a truly liberal, humanistic approach to the study of man. Those of you acquainted with the work of Professor Di Pietro, either as colleague or student, will agree that he has continually striven to integrate the finest traditions of the humanities with the rigorous scientific approach to language characteristic of the major portion of this century. Tonight we honor not only Professor Di Pietro's personal achievements in linguistics and languages, but also his dedicated teaching career; and in the spirit of this evening's 'humanistic' theme, I would like to recall to your minds what Xenophon so well pointed out long ago:

INTRODUCTION

'Όσαι δ'ἐν ἀνθρώποις ἀρεταὶ λέγονται, σκοπούμενος
εὑρήσει πάσας μαθήσει τε καὶ μελέτῃ αὐξανομένας.

'If you consider what are called the virtues in
mankind, you will find that in all cases their
growth is assisted by education and cultivation.'
                    XENOPHON, *Memorabilia* II. 6, 39.

One of the duties of the recipient of the Mellon
Award is to present during the time of his tenure the
Andrew W. Mellon Lecture. Professor Di Pietro will
this evening give the first Mellon Lecture, entitled
'Language as Human Creation.' Ladies and Gentle-
men, it is my privilege to introduce to you the
Professor who will inaugurate this series of Dis-
tinguished Mellon Lectures, Robert J. Di Pietro.

Language as Human Creation

Robert J. Di Pietro

First Andrew W. Mellon Distinguished Lecture

January 23, 1976

1. *Introduction.* Creativity is a very large word. Even if we limit it to the context of language, it is still unwieldy. Nevertheless, linguists have become fond of talking about how people are creative with language. Within the boundaries of generative grammar, we have come to think of linguistic creativity as that property of grammatical systems which provides for the production of infinitely varied sentences, each within a proper context and each conveying a meaning. I have already suggested (Di Pietro 1970) that the generation of well-formed sentences by a speaker is only one kind of creativity with language. I chose to call it 'innovation' and I now liken it to the kinds of innovations a composer might make within a pre-scribed harmonic structure and tempo assignment. The musical inventions of Johann Sebastian Bach are recognizable to anyone who is familiar with the framework in which Bach composed. However, there is more to creativity than innovation, in music as well as in language. As human beings we can create not only the score—both musical and verbal—but also the constraints we choose to impose on our creative activity. Just as Bach can be out of context, so may a sentence which follows the grammatical con-straints of a language sound strangely discordant if uttered in a context where one expects to have the rules of another language applied. Our creative capacity is sufficiently great to enable us to change and re-form the systems which generate our sentences. Language is very much a human creation—even though it may share traits with other systems of com-munication on earth. In its flexibility, its efficiency to convey thought and to establish rapport, and its pro-vision for socialization, it surpasses by far any other vehicle of verbal exchange in the world. My goals in this lecture are, first, to discuss some of the broad implications of human creativity with language;

second, to relate linguistics to the humanistic pursuits of studies in literature; and, finally, to suggest how both linguistics and literature can contribute to the teaching of foreign languages. This last mentioned goal is of central importance to the School of Languages and Linguistics of Georgetown University, dedicated as it is to the study of all aspects of language.

2. *Language as grammar.* Given the enormity of language, there are several possible ways to study it as a science. Linguistics, which considers itself the discipline most concerned with human verbalization, has chosen to do it grammatically. A grammar of a language becomes, for the linguist, a theory of that language. While this grammar-theory correlation has stimulated much scholarly activity, it is worth considering some of its limitations. First of all, grammar relates to form, not to content. We linguists speak eloquently of how meaning is being structured in language but even in the most semantically based theories, the outcome is always expressed in terms of sentence-forms. We use our rules to accept or reject utterances we actually hear or postulate as likely to be heard. If the output of our rules is significantly distorted, then we reformulate the rules.

There is another ramification of language seen as

grammar. It is the assumption that language performance is motivated solely by underlying thought
or mental concepts of some sort. While individual
thought (which, incidentally, we understand badly)
might generate some of what we say, the view that it
is the sole generator neatly cuts off any reference to
other variables involved in communication. Among
these other variables one might include the wish to
dominate an interaction and the attempt to portray a
self which takes a number of different configurations.

Dingwall (1975:38–9) gives in succinct form the
model of communication which is either in wide
acceptance or remains unquestioned by language
specialists. This model is traditionally depicted as two
human heads interconnected by a line representing
the passage of a concept from one head to the other
through the medium of language. Dingwall not only
provides an illustration but he adds, quite accurately,
that 'theoretical linguistics today, as in the past, re-
gards as its principal concern the nature of the trans-
duction between meaning and sound' (Dingwall
1975:39). Such a model has accommodated much
theorizing and research activity, especially among the
so-called psycholinguists. It does not, however, provide for the possibility that either of the fictionalized
individuals interlocked in communication by a thread
of meaning-bearing sound might wish to influence

the direction of thought or action of the other. To be sure, when someone utters the word *tree*, the sounds remind the hearer of a plant which has bark, branches, leaves, and roots. At the same time, the hearer may be concerned with why his partner in the speech act has chosen to evoke this image. Why has he or she put into operation such a complex and finely tuned apparatus of speech generation to utter the word *tree*? Whatever the reasons, the hearer will react in accordance with a personal interpretation of the illocutionary force of the utterance. The word may have been uttered in a phonetics laboratory before a sonograph. Or it may have been shouted in a dense forest to warn of a falling tree. To be sure, the context will figure importantly in how the hearer will react. As a student in a phonetics course, he may make a few scribbles in a notebook. The lumberjack in the forest may simply jump aside. The outcome of a speech act cannot be fully predicted, however, because each communicant is a complex human being who brings a personal interpretation to each situation. The student may not write anything down and the lumberjack may not jump aside.

3. *Metaphor.* As a necessary preparation to exploring the ways language functions in interpersonal communication, let us consider the source of linguistic creativity in the individual. I would like to propose that poetic force is the key innate property of language. Whatever locus this poetic force may have in the brain, it is born with each of us and manifests itself through the various metaphorical operations. Metaphor, the relating of disparate objects and ideas to find a communality among them, appears to inspire not only verbal strategies but even grammatical systems. I recall that my own daughter at age two and one-half classified animals into four simple categories: birds, bugs, butterflies, and bow-wows. I probably shall never be able fully to understand the distinctive features she found to establish these categories, but here are likely candidates: birds are creatures that fly, to which you cannot get too close; these creatures also make noises; bugs are very small creatures that move around and allow you to get close; butterflies are also small but they fly and if you try to catch them, they flutter away; bow-wows have four legs, come in various sizes, and sometimes make loud noises. Within this four-way division, houseflies were classed with butterflies, an association that most adult speakers of English would certainly reject. Horses were bow-wows, along with dogs. So were cats.

I cannot really say how long this simple classification of the animal kingdom lasted, but as the child's world of experience expanded, it was lost. Eve Clark (1975) has discussed similar groupings among young children under the title of 'overextensions'. But there is more to it than simply an unbridled correlating of features. Like other children, my child easily accepted the metaphorical representation of things for the things themselves. When shown a picture of a rabbit, she would say, most naturally, 'that's a rabbit' and not 'that's a picture of a rabbit'. Being able to accept metaphors as realities is important for the functioning of creativity in all sorts of human endeavors. The flower we call a *daisy* is the result of someone seeing in its arrangement of center and petals a configuration resembling an eye—the day's eye. The making of *daisy* into a proper name results from a second application of the metaphorical process in which the name of the flower serves as the starting point and its original derivation is ignored. Building metaphors on metaphors is common in all languages. For better or worse, we begin to believe our own metaphors. Thus the poet Langston Hughes offers this touching but sad definition of the word 'misery': 'Misery,' he writes, 'is when you hear on the radio that the neighborhood you live in is a slum but you always thought it was home' (Hughes 1969).

Some effort has been made to seek universals in the ways humans perceive the world and derive language from their perceptions. Wallace Chafe, in his book *Meaning and the Structure of Language* (see

Chafe 1970:85ff.), asserts that it is universally human to know that certain animals bark. Along with members of the genus *Canis* he includes the seal, as animals that emit a barking sound. Such an association is probably quite important for Chafe's belief that verbs are central to the sentence. The verb *bark* thus attracts the nouns *dog* and *seal* just as the verb *swarm* attracts the plural noun *bees* as a potential subject. While such may be the case in English, this association is by no means universal. In German, for example, seals howl (*heulen*). One Spanish speaker told me that the sound made by seals resembled crying or sobbing. While it is possible that human perceptions are somehow constrained by our physical structure, we are far from being able to predict how these perceptions will result in language. The poetic imagination of people is a powerful tool.

Metaphor—with all its resulting figures of speech —is well known to literary analysts who have supplied a wealth of documentation of it through the ages. Underlying its rich variety is the simple extension of semantic features from one universe of discourse to another. In a favorite poem of mine, the *Laudes creaturarum* of Francis of Assisi, natural phenomena are discussed with family kinship terms. When Francis speaks of the sun, it is *frate sole* 'brother sun', and the moon is *sora luna* 'sister moon'.

Even death becomes a relative. If ever there should be a patron saint of the ecological movement, Francis of Assisi would certainly qualify. He makes us feel the closeness of our existence with the world and its life around us. He is also careful not to violate the grammatical constraints of Italian by prefacing words which are masculine with *frate* and words which are feminine with *sora* or *madre*.

Umberto Saba, a modern Italian poet, uses a similar technique in a poem about his wife (*A mia moglie*, in the collection *Canzoniere* of 1921). Even though Saba likens her to animals which are not often recipients of human traits, his poetic skill is so great that we can believe him when he says at the conclusion of his poem that he finds his loved one again and again 'in all the females of all the peaceful animals that come close to God' ('. . . *in tutte le femmine di tutti i sereni animali che avvicinano a Dio*'). Over 700 years may separate Francis of Assisi from Umberto Saba but their poetic creation is ageless. It stems from the same innate property of human language that is in all of us. To those among us who are able to be highly productive with their poetic competence we give the title 'poet'. The poetic competence which is, perhaps, more receptive than productive in the rest of us is no less important. Without it, the productivity of the poet would go unrecognized.

Evidence continues to mount that grammar itself is metaphorical in origin. Children not only learn to speak but they become linguistically acculturated to perceive aspects of what they are saying as patterned. Oppositions are essential to the creation of grammatical pattern. As Clark (1975:87) points out, citing some earlier research by Donaldson and Balfour, children of three and four years may learn the words *more* and *less* before recognizing them as opposites. Grammar seems to become more significant for the speaker as a socializing force than as a representation of his linguistic competence. Sociolinguists interested in variation have amply illustrated how grammar reflects social organization. As sophisticated as we are, linguists of all theoretical convictions are no more immune from metaphorizing than were our forebears who first established the categories of noun, verb, adverb, and adjective. Today, each linguistic school has its favorite metaphors in which it strongly believes and which it will defend. To take a contemporary example, we find generativists describing the sentence as having a tree structure, complete with branches and nested constructions. 'Pruning' is one of the operations they use to transform these trees into other shapes. The metaphors of earlier linguists are soundly denounced as fictions. The fate of the phoneme is a good example. Some efforts to rescue this concept from complete disfavor have been made by linguists who add a qualifier to it, such as 'autonomous' or 'systematic'.

4. *On change and evolution in language.* In trying to comprehend the range of creativity in human language, it is inevitable that we consider language evolution and language change. The subject of the origin of language has long been a taboo topic for professional linguists. The early theories proposed were so far from adequate that they easily fell under fatuous labels which mocked their basic notions. The 'bow-wow' and the 'ding-dong' theories are still mentioned in derision in introductory linguistic textbooks. Recently, however, the subject has been approached once again—this time by investigators armed with pertinent and numerous data from disciplines as diverse as developmental psychology, physical and social anthropology, sociology, and the education of the deaf. Last year there appeared an excellent book edited by Roger Wescott (Wescott 1974) which draws from much data to support a gestural foundation for human speech. A recent (Fall, 1975) meeting of the New York Academy of Sciences was dedicated entirely to the subject and was attended by a host of scholars who, while not in agreement about gestural origins, contributed much to the ultimate solving of the puzzle.

However language originated, it is clear that historical linguists have not distinguished between change and evolution in their published work. The argument presented by Weinreich, Labov, and Herzog (1968) that language is in constant flux in any speech community brings into question the Saussurean dichotomy of synchrony vs. diachrony. It does not result in any questioning of the usual procedure in historical linguistics of charting shifts and changes in phonology, syntax, and lexicon. It challenges only the way in which the charting is done and the omission of sociological data. In the most recent issue of *Language*, Charles N. Li (1975) analyzes Mandarin Chinese and concludes that the language drifted away from a VO to an OV topology. As informative as such studies can be, they offer no insight into the evolutionary processes of language. On the basis of what is known from historical linguistics, there is nothing to suppose that language as spoken by Indo-Europeans or Sino-Tibetans four thousand years ago was any lower on an evolutionary scale than contemporary languages. There is no doubt that humans of four thousand years ago had the same anatomical structure, the same brain, and the same compulsion to organize socially as we have today. If a socially sensitive transformational grammar can work to describe contemporary languages, it should also work for languages spoken by humans in ancient times. There is no reason to think any differently about the matter once we recognize the limitations of what we are doing. Human creativity with language, taken in its larger sense, is tied intimately to our physical, psychic, and social nature. As long as we have not evolved in any of these domains, our language has not undergone an evolutionary change. It would be far more accurate to speak of rearrangement or innovation in language structure as the customary object of study by historical linguists. No meaningful inquiry into the evolution of language can be made without seeing language as one of several communication systems and expanding one's range of research to include the work of specialists in other fields, as did Wescott and the New York Academy of Sciences, mentioned earlier.

I have brought up this matter of language evolution in part to emphasize the limitations of a grammar-based linguistics. Trying to understand how language evolved by charting the changes undergone in the grammar of a language is like trying to formulate a theory about transportation, with all its implications for society, by comparing a contemporary automobile engine with earlier versions of the same engine. As far as the origin of language is concerned, it would not be farfetched to postulate that the poetic force which motivates human verbalization today also figured prominently in the first act of human speech. This idea is not a new one. The Italian scholar Giambattista Vico thought of it in the eighteenth century (see Bergin and Fisch 1968). The metaphorical power of language must have been just as critical for that first band of humans who discovered it eons ago as it is for each human child born today who rediscovers it on the path to maturation.

5. *Roles and verbal strategies.* In our study of linguistic creativity we have to entertain a very basic question: why do people speak to each other at all? To be sure, we speak to exchange information—but there are many ways to do that besides entering into conversation with other people. We can build repositories of information in books and computer data banks. We can post signs, as we do for traffic control on busy highways. We can print diagrams as we do on the backs of radios and TV sets. A book, a sign, and a diagram do transmit information but in using them we become passive participants in the communication process. In fact, as our society accumulates more information, we become ever more passive.

There are still some good reasons for speaking and entering into conversations. Insofar as we are social beings, we find it necessary to use language to articulate our existence. Whether we use sounds or sign language, our personalities are verbal expressions of ourselves. With time we develop distinct strategies of speech to assure that our personalities will emerge intact from any verbal encounter. Through the enactment of these strategies we get others to play roles which reciprocate the one we wish to play. As Arnold Mysior puts it, roles are 'circumscribed behavior patterns . . . governed by the need to entertain relations with others' (see Mysior 1975ms:416). By a number of different devices and conventions, we come to recognize the role-types that are playable in our society. In Medieval and Renaissance times, for example, the role of the court jester or fool was clearly circumscribed. Dressed in distinctive garb, the jester played the part of the critic, the one who could make offensive but accurate remarks about his patron and other persons in power. His status as a fool protected him from ostracism. This stylized fool's role has evolved today into the stand-up nightclub comedian who can make caustic and insulting remarks about celebrities or persons in his audience with impunity. Philip A. Dennis (1975), in his study of role playing in a Mexican village, ascribes to the social drunk the same kind of license to criticize and insult. The drunk and the court fool are 'anti-roles' insofar as they serve to relieve the pressures of a restrictive society without threatening its structure.

It would not be difficult to find some correlation between the incidence of drunkenness, with its ensuing offenses against social organization, and the repressive societies of the world. Rather than go into the social implications of this particular train of thought, I prefer to direct attention to the nature of the language employed. Drunkenness slurs speech, to be sure, but since the patterns of sounds are different in every language, does slurred speech manifest itself uniformly? While the question is still open, I feel that slurred speech is not the same in all languages and the key to recognizing it is to be found in understanding the pattern of sounds that is specific to each language. The student who has learned French, German, or Italian may be quite taken by hearing the first drunken performance in those languages. There are many instances of inebriated speech in literature to which the language teacher can draw attention, in an effort to familiarize the student with it.

But there is a more basic point in this that I would like to make. We all feel the need to criticize from time to time, while not wishing to become a fool or a drunk to do it. We have evolved certain verbal strategies in order to give criticism without leaving ourselves open to counterattack. These strategies often take the form of an opener in conversation. In English, we have a number of self-protective openers to giving a criticism: *I hate to say this to you, but* . . . or *I hate being the one to tell you this* . . . or *I don't know how to tell you this* . . . . This last-mentioned is obviously a lie since the critic disclaims any ability to criticize but then goes ahead and does it. Studying the strategic function of language would be of little consequence if all languages contained equivalent expressions. As far as I can determine, each language has its own set of verbal strategies. In German, for example, the disclaiming opener may take the form of something like: *Es mag zwar dumm klingen, aber* . . . (literally, 'it might sound dumb, but . . .'). But will it actually sound dumb to make the criticism? No matter, since the critic can now feel properly protected from counterassaults. These disclaimers are verbal equivalents to the fool's cape and the drunk's stagger. It is too cumbersome for us to resort to a costume change or to an affectation of slurred speech every time we wish to hurl an insult or make an offensive remark. It is far more efficient to protect ourselves verbally. We can slip in and out of the critic's role with speed and ease by a careful choice of words.

Linguistics has yet to incorporate into its study the fact that language use is dramatic. People do not spend their waking hours simply paying lip service to grammatical constraints, to semantic categories, or to social structure. Even the poorest and least educated among us is capable of finding a meaning to life that makes what is exchanged verbally with other people personal and significant beyond all present analytical procedures. As we go through our days we take part in a drama in which we attempt to write our own scripts and to cast others in roles which are pleasing to us. Depending on the day or the time of day, we may wish to be cooperating partners, consolers, plaintiffs, defendants, vendors, buyers, and lovers. Since each of these roles requires a counterpart in order to be successfully carried off, we develop skills to lead other persons to play the complementing role. We also develop counter-strategies to avoid being cast in roles we do not wish to play. The woman who enters the clothing store, for example, has cast herself as a potential buyer in the eyes of the sales staff of that store. The opening sales-pitch may be a simple *Can I help you?* If the woman wishes to be a buyer, there are a number of answers she can give to show her intention: *Can you show me something in black leather?* or *What do you have in black leather?*, for example. There is also a strategy to avoid being a buyer. Every speaker of American English knows it: *Just looking, thank you.* Since buying and selling can be such an important part of our everyday activity, it is crucial that our students learn equivalent strategies in the foreign languages they are studying.

The drama of everyday life is made complicated by the differing styles employed to activate verbal strategies. Every person functioning in a society is aware of the differences of age, sex, social standing, and the other social markings appropriate to that society. The verbal strategies employed reflect these differences. To give an example from my own experience, my daughter, having reached age six, employed a child's version of a strategy to avoid implication in a naughty deed. Upon discovering some minor mischief that had been done, I exclaimed that I knew who did it and half-seriously threatened punishment. My daughter, wishing to find out if I really knew who the guilty party was but not wanting to point the finger of accusation directly at herself, responded with: 'Was it December or June?'. This strategy could only work within my family. December is the month of her birthday and June is that of her younger brother. By not naming names and by referring to birth months, she cushioned herself from punishment. She neatly reminded me, via this use of metonymy, that she and her brother were my children and therefore some consideration should be made of that fact if I intended to punish anybody. While I think that my daughter is very bright, I do not think that such sophistication in a six-year-old is necessarily unusual. Other parents can most likely cite their own examples of skilful verbal strategies invented by their children.

It is unfortunate that psycholinguistic studies of child language acquisition are so overly committed to development of grammar. How good it would be to know if verbal strategies are acquired in any set way. My own suspicion is that they are products of each child's poetic creativity, just as metaphors are.

6. *Linguistics and the study of literature.* It is regrettable that the paths of linguistics and literary analysis have wandered so far apart in recent times. We should praise those representatives of both camps who have tried to maintain a rapprochement of some sort between the two disciplines. Of course, if we go back far enough in time, we will find that almost all language specialists worked with literature. In the nineteenth century these specialists called their activity 'philology' and were proud of the insights they gained into the workings of language from literature. Now that the contemporary linguist can look to anthropology, sociology, and psychology for new inspiration, the bonds tying him to literary analysis have weakened. Nowadays, the currents of influence between linguistics and literary studies flow almost exclusively in the direction of the latter. There are scholars who actively apply linguistic concepts to literary analysis, ranging all the way from prosody to stylistics. Yet, it is also true that the linguist has become an interloper in the field of literature. The impact of his work ranges all the way from eager acceptance to total rejection. The attitude of Quentin G. Kraft, writing in *College English* on science and poetics (see Kraft 1975), is typical. While Kraft welcomes the holistic and integrative emphasis which structuralism carries with it, he rejects the pretense of imposing scientific method on the study of literature and art. He quotes Hulme as saying, 'A perfect cube looks stable in comparison with the flux of appearance, but one might be pardoned if one felt no particular interest in the eternity of a cube' (Kraft 1975:168). We come closest to structuring humans, Kraft goes on to say, when we place them in boxes, cells, and coffins.

Paula Johnson (1975) has characterized the linguistic approach to literature as one in which the work of art is treated as an information-bearing corpus. The task of analysis becomes one of re-encoding this corpus into rules and providing for the paraphrasing of its textual content in other sentences. Johnson discusses some of the alternative ways to 'understand' a work of art: (1) one can situate it in some literary genre, (2) interpret its message or allegorical worth, and (3) view it as part of a social movement of some kind.

Fortunately, there are some indications that literary analysis can and does contribute to linguistic theory. Liane Norman (1975), for example, provides a discussion of redundancy in literary texts as a device to achieve the compassion or interest of the reader. Redundancy, which is usually dismissed by the linguist as a surface phenomenon of language, has apparently great strategic importance in communicating through a text. If we are ever to formulate a statement of language use, we must certainly include redundancy as a verbal strategy.

That the literary text is more than a number of sentences strung together in an extended corpus is clearly shown by Ursula Oomen's (1975) study on poetic communication. A poem can be looked upon as a particular kind of speech act in which the poet communicates with an unknown reader (or listener). The deictic function of pronouns, however, can be quite unlike that of speech acts in which both addresser and addressee are present and the form of the act is not literary. The first person pronoun 'I', for example, can mean the poet himself or some person mentioned in the poem or even some fictionalized narrator. Performative verbs such as *ask* and *tell* are either stated explicitly or implied by the poet at different critical points. While poets employ many communicational devices and not just the rules of grammar in writing a poem, they are careful to avoid restrictions which would contain their poetic performances within particular spatial or temporal frames of reference in everyday life. As a result, poetry has what Oomen calls a 'representational character' which makes it capable of being repeated and enjoyed as a speech performance over and over again.

I am certain that people will go on disagreeing about the purpose of literature for a long time to come. At least we can agree that literature is a legitimate use of language and one which deserves the linguist's attention. Its legitimacy derives from a universal human need to use language to capture thoughts and discharge emotional tensions. Not all thoughts can be captured in expository prose and even the best scientific writing has a poetic cast. When we are truly touched by a poem, we experience an understanding of things which would otherwise escape statement. I am reminded of some lines by ee cummings, who made this last point much better than I: '. . . who pays any attention/ to the syntax of things/ will never wholly kiss you/ . . . /the best gesture of my brain is less than your eyelids flutter which says/ we are for each other . . . / for lifes not a paragraph/ and death . . . is no parenthesis.'

7. *Linguistics and literature in the language classroom.* Having spoken about some contributions to linguistic theory which are derivable from a study of literature, I would now like to make some remarks about an endeavor which relates to both fields, namely, the teaching of languages. The research activities of the past decade have concentrated on language teaching at beginning levels and have been largely within the framework of psychology and psycholinguistics. We have learned something about how young children learn languages. We have witnessed the publication of new texts which purport to be 'student-centered' and the proliferation of testing programs, each new one claiming greater efficiency than the ones before it. Teachers accustom themselves to speaking about 'behavioral objectives'. More and more, the learning of a foreign language is equated to the acquiring of new 'cognitive skills' and the developing of 'positive attitudes' towards the foreign culture.

Literature has become lost somewhere under this wave of scientific consciousness. Yet the student who truly likes to read might still feel that there is more to gain from a people's literature than examples of how their cultural system operates. In fact, once we go beyond those early years of language instruction, the presentation of literature remains the major classroom activity. Rather than wait for the behavioral scientists to tell us what to do in our advanced courses, I propose that we reaffirm the relevancy of literature in learning a second language, even at elementary levels in our universities. The question before us should not be what to put in place of literature but how to make literary texts better serve the goal of teaching the language.

One answer to this question is to approach the teaching of languages as a dramaturgical activity. The use of language in everyday life is not unlike the performing of a script to a play. Life-drama is played in earnest by actors who move from role to role in different settings. The teacher as dramatist should be expected to address the potential strategic worth of sentences first and their grammatical structure second. French expressions such as *j'ai faim, j'ai soif*, and *j'ai froid*, for example, are more than quaint grammatical structures used by native speakers to set themselves off from the English-speaking tourists who visit their country. A speaker of French says *j'ai faim* in a number of different circumstances, with an aim to achieve a number of different goals. Beyond its grammatical meaning of 'I'm hungry', the speaker of French could intend it as a signal to co-workers to stop for lunch. He could also mean it as a question:

'When is dinner ready?' or as a command: 'Give me something to eat', or simply as a cue to what he is going to do: 'I'm going to eat now'. Each of these meanings is correlated with the role being played by the speaker. From this correlation between context and role the 'strategic value' of the utterance emerges. A foreman who has observed his men working hard all morning might say *j'ai faim* as a signal to stop working. From the mouth of a man who is playing lord and master in his home, it becomes a command to put dinner on the table.

I suspect that the desire to play a role in life-drama is far more important in motivating conversational speech than the compulsion to share information. Surely the person who says *j'ai faim* is doing more than declaring that he feels hunger. Even in those speech events where the conveying of information seems to be the overriding concern, such as in giving a lecture, the implementation of strategies is critical. If I were to give this lecture in a monotone, showing no major commitment to what I am saying, I would be failing in my role as a lecturer. You, as an audience, might demonstrate that I am failing by a number of strategies—most of them nonverbal—such as shuffling your feet, yawning, gazing off in a direction away from me as lecturer, and so on. The strategies of attentiveness may even differ from culture to culture and from social stratum to social stratum. Whatever they are, they represent elements of communicative competence which are necessary for behavior in groups such as this one.

To return to the strategies employed by individuals in small group interaction, literature represents a great storehouse from which to draw prime examples for the learners. Scripts from plays are natural sources of verbal strategies. Let me take an example from opera which qualifies as musical drama. Johann Strauss, in his delightful operetta, *Die Fledermaus*, gives his female lead, Rosalinde, some very effective and entertaining lines. There is a scene where Alfred, who is Rosalinde's incessant suitor, has managed to place himself at her table, dressed in her husband's evening robe. Rosalinde's husband, Eisenstein, has just left the house to begin serving a jail term. Frank, the warden, comes upon the scene to escort Eisenstein personally to prison. From what he sees, Frank must assume that Alfred is Eisenstein. This state of affairs is, of course, embarrassing to Rosalinde. If she tells the truth, that Alfred is not her husband, she will be scandalized. The only other apparent solution is to lie and say that Alfred is her husband. In the aria she sings, she neither confirms nor denies Alfred's connubial status but instead lets Frank come to his own conclusions. 'What do you think of me, sir,' she exclaims, 'would I be sitting here with a stranger? You, sir, are questioning my honor! Who else but my husband would be sitting here with me so late?' The word she uses for 'husand', incidentally, is *Gatte*, rather than the more intimate German expression *Mann*. By doing so, she not only underscores the social distance between her and the lower-class Frank but also builds an aura of propriety for the setting. The full text reads as follows:

> *Mein Herr, was dächten Sie von mir.*
> *säss ich mit einem Fremden hier,*
> *das wär doch sonderbar!*
> *Mit solchen Zweifeln treten da*
> *Sie wahrlich meiner Ehr' zu nah:*
> *beleid'gen denn diese Situation.*
> *Spricht denn diese Situation*
> *hier nicht klar und deutlich schon?*
> *Mit mir so spät*
> *im tête-à-tête,*
> *ganz traulich und allein,*
> *in dem Kostüm, so ganz intim,*
> *kann nur allein der Gatte sein!*

Indeed, Rosalinde lets the situation speak for itself in reaffirming her projected role as faithful wife. For the innovative teacher of German, this vignette could be used to teach some of the grammar involved. In the first three lines, the subjunctive mood is used repeatedly to establish the strategy of 'letting the situation speak for itself' (*dächten, säss, wär*). Other contexts could be postulated by the teacher to give students the opportunity to re-employ the subjunctive with other verbs to achieve the same strategy.

The writers of opera *libretti* often achieve great heights of strategic impact with single words. Two examples of this are from Charles Gounod's *Faust* and Giacomo Puccini's *Tosca*. The librettists for *Faust*, Barbier and Carré, start the opera with the aging scholar alone in his study. The first word old Faust utters dramatically sums up the desperation of a useless quest for scholarship: '*Rien!*'—'Nothing'. His whole life has been wasted. He has languished unilluminated. He goes on: '*Je ne vois rien!—Je ne sais rien!*' A more likely candidate for the devil's workshop could hardly be found. Librettists Giuseppe Giacosa and Luigi Illica are able to have Puccini's heroine Tosca sum up all her scorn for the villainous Scarpia with one word: '*Quanto!*'—'How much!' On the surface, Tosca is asking Scarpia how much he will take to free her boyfriend, Mario, from further torture as a political prisoner. The strategic value of what she asks is much greater. Tosca senses Scarpia's lust for her. Her terse question is delivered with an intonational contour loaded with irony. This is not the *quanto* of the textbook dialog where Signora X buys a kilo of pasta at the corner grocer's. This is a *quanto* one uses in conveying great moral disgust. Scarpia's retort is classic in its simplicity: '*Quanto?*' (he repeats the word, this time with a mock questioning intonation). Tosca does not elaborate very much: '*Il prezzo!*'—'The price!' The professor of Italian could have the students listen to the opera and then prepare simple dialogs using these lines in a number of different settings, e.g. offering a bribe to an official, preparing to haggle over a price in a small shop, or bargaining in an open market, with much surrounding noise. Another exercise, at a higher level of language instruction, could be worked around an analysis of why Scarpia repeats Tosca's question. Reading on in the libretto, we find the villain hesitating, feigning dedication to high ideals: '*a donna bella non mi vendo . . . a prezzo di moneta . . . no! no!*'— He wouldn't think of selling himself to a beautiful woman, at least not for money!

Gaetano Donizetti's opera, *The Elixir of Love* (*L'elisir d'amore*), provides an interesting illustration of the use of pronouns to convey an imbalance in personal relations. The heroine, Adina, in order to discourage courting by Nemorino, keeps him on a lower social status. Her use of the familiar form of address *tu*, right from the start of the opera, contrasts sharply with his respectful but warm *voi* when

speaking to her (the Italian spoken at the time would
make a three-way contrast between *tu*—for intimates
or social inferiors—*voi*—for respectful but not distant
address—and *lei*—for strangers). Toward the end of
the opera, Adina's feelings about the young man
change. To show her new-found affection for Nemorino, she would be expected to shift to *tu*. But since
she has already chosen to use *tu* to keep him at a social
distance, there is no shift to make. Her solution to
this problem in communication is to lead Nemorino
to change his *voi* to *tu* when speaking to her. This
she does by changing reference to herself from *ci*
(us) to *mi* (me). '*Sàppilo, alfin,*' she says, '*tu mi sei
caro.*' 'Know it at last, you are dear to me'. Just before
this line, she prepares Nemorino for the shift by
saying, '*la tua vita ci è cara*', i.e., 'your life is dear to us'.
Although the objective pronoun remains that of the
socially distant first person plural ('to us'), the content
of the message is warm and affectionate. Nemorino can
at last shift to *tu* in addressing Adina: '*tu m'ami, oh
gioia inesprimibile!*' 'You love me, oh great joy!' (see
Di Pietro 1975 for a discussion of this point in detail).
One use in the classroom of this kind of dialog would
be as a guide to when and how to shift to informal
levels of address. An assignment could be given to
prepare a different dialog showing a similar shift in
intimacy by both grammatical form and message con-

tent. Several students could be asked to collaborate on preparing the dialog.

Moving to the field of Spanish letters, we encounter Calderón's *El gran teatro del mundo*, in which God is cast as the great playwright who assigns roles to people. This *auto sacramental* has many possibilities for classroom dramaturgy. Valle-Inclán's play, *Sacrilegio*, offers a clear example of yet another type of phenomenon in role-playing, namely, the difference between a life-role and a situational role. In this play, a band of thieves has condemned one of its members to execution for what they consider excess avarice. Frasquito, the condemned thief, requests a priest to hear his final confession. The thieves have no intention to honor Frasquito's request but one of them does disguise himself as a priest. Frasquito proceeds to show such repentance for evil past deeds that the other thieves begin to sway from their decision to execute him. The counterfeit priest and the penitent thief are playing situational roles—those of confessor and confessant. The audience is dramatically and suddenly reminded that the extended life-roles being portrayed are evil ones by a gunshot blast from one of the unswayed thieves which kills Frasquito. The classroom teacher should be able to find someone who would like to be a Frasquito and take upon himself the task of convincing a disbelieving audience that he is possessed of an altruistic nature (I am indebted to my colleague Estelle Irizarry, of the Spanish department of Georgetown University, for these examples).

In a dramaturgical approach to language teaching, our attention is inevitably drawn to the classroom as a locale. For some time now, teachers have tried to transform the classroom into a place which would be somehow associated with the language being taught. They find large posters to place on the walls and they move the desks and chairs around to make various patterns. Some teachers use props and even costumes. In one case I read about, a French teacher dressed up like *le Roi Soleil*, replete with curled wig, long, flowing coat, and buckle shoes. Perhaps teachers are pushed to such extremes by textbook writers who like to locate conversations in public places like cafés, hotel lobbies, railroad stations, post offices, museums, and libraries. Public places are easy to envision and they tend to constrain the type of information that is likely to be conveyed. But try as we may, the classroom ultimately fails as a place. Its 'place-ness' is real only as a classroom in which a teacher meets with students and they have a language lesson. But while the classroom may fail as a place, it is perfectly adequate as a performing space. Verbal strategies and role-playing are only superficially connected to a setting. We need only an empty space to engage our student-actors in the various roles they are to play. In fact, props, posters, and costumes might even be distracting to them. Commitment to the lines of a dialog must come from within.

8. *Concluding remarks.* I have drawn your attention to a number of interrelated subjects in order to get at an understanding of creativity in language. I began by making a distinction between innovation and the broader acts of creativity. Sentence generation was seen as a demonstration of the innovative power of grammar. Judgments as to the well-formedness of utterances and all the operations of syntax, whether or not they are motivated by semantics, remain bound to a form-oriented paradigm. As long as we are grammar-bound in our work, linguists and language teachers alike will never transcend their structuralist period and never seriously concern themselves with the other aspects of creativity in language. One of my contentions is that metaphor is a greater creative force than grammatical innovation. Through the several processes of metaphor we create not only new sentences but grammar itself. The manipulation of language in conversational strategies and role enactment is also a product of language creativity.

Teachers of languages must confront human creativity in all its ramifications. To learn a new language is not the equivalent of learning the grammar of that language. It is not a special case of data processing, as some linguists might claim. It is much more. Giving increased importance to literary studies in the foreign language curriculum is essential if some understanding is to be reached of how the speakers of a language use it to portray interactional roles, to structure conversational scripts, and to do the many things humans do everyday. Grammar cannot be expanded to incorporate the many verbal strategies created by people because grammar is built around a concern for the form of what is said. As linguists, we have had a game theory approach to language. Our concern has been with discovering what the rules of the game are. Now we need to go beyond game rules to game 'plan'. We need to understand how people invoke language to succeed in the playing of a dialog.

This evening, I have not spoken about paralanguage, proxemics, or any of the other nonverbal ways in which we communicate as humans. However, a study of verbal language could not be complete without considering everything else that goes into a speech act. The most likely approach to a global study of human communication, with the evidence gathered so far, appears to be one in which verbal and nonverbal codes contribute to similar communicational ends, rather than having nonverbal behavior considered as an incidental accompaniment to verbal language.

In closing, I cannot resist drawing your attention to our own behavior at this event. We have been bound to each other as lecturer and audience. I as lecturer have been allowed to do all the talking while you as the 'lectured-at' have been permitted only to display signs of audience membership and, hopefully, some attentiveness. As lecturer, I have the responsibility to close the event. You will observe that my way of preparing you for the end of my talking was to use the expression 'in closing'. You have now been cued to provide the behavior audiences usually provide at the end of a lecture. I am also aware that applause at the end of a lecture can be interpreted just as much as relief that the event has been concluded as approval of what has been said. Thank you.

REFERENCES

Bergin, T.G. and M.H. Fisch, trans. 1968. *The new science of Giambattista Vico*. Ithaca, Cornell University Press.

Chafe, Wallace. 1970. *Meaning and the structure of language*. Chicago, The University of Chicago Press.

Clark, Eve. 1975. 'Knowledge, context, and strategy in the acquisition of meaning.' In: *Georgetown University Round Table on Languages and Linguistics 1975*. Edited by Daniel P. Dato. Washington, D.C., Georgetown University Press. 77-98.

Dennis, Philip A. 1975. 'The role of the drunk in a Oaxacan village.' *American Anthropologist* 77.856-63.

Dingwall, William O. 1975. 'The species-specificity of speech.' In: *Georgetown University Round Table on Languages and Linguistics 1975*. Edited by Daniel P. Dato. Washington, D.C., Georgetown University Press. 17-62.

Di Pietro, Robert J. 1970. 'Notes on "innovation" and "creativity".' In: *Georgetown University Papers on Languages and Linguistics*, Number 1. Washington, D.C., Georgetown University Press. 30-33.

———. 1975. 'Speech protocols and verbal strategies in the teaching of Italian.' *The Canadian Modern Language Review* 32.24-38.

REFERENCES

Hughes, Langston. 1969. *Black misery*. New York, Paul S. Eriksson.

Johnson, Paula. 1975. 'Getting acquainted with a poem.' *College English* 37.358-67.

Kraft, Quentin G. 1975. 'Science and poetics, old and new.' *College English* 37.167-75.

Li, Charles N. 1975. 'Synchrony vs. diachrony in language structure.' *Language* 51.873-86.

Mysior, Arnold. 1975. 'Society—a very large system.' Unpublished manuscript. Washington, D.C., Georgetown University.

Norman, Liane. 1975. 'Risk and redundancy.' *PMLA* 90.285-91.

Oomen, Ursula. 1975. 'On some elements of poetic communication.' In: *Georgetown University Papers on Languages and Linguistics*, Number 11. Edited by Robert J. Di Pietro. Washington, D.C., Georgetown University Press. 60-8.

Weinreich, Uriel, William Labov, and M. Herzog. 1968. 'Empirical foundations for a theory of language change.' In: *Directions for historical linguistics*. Edited by W.P. Lehmann and Y. Malkiel. Austin, University of Texas Press. 95-188.

Wescott, Roger, ed. 1974. *Language origins*. Silver Spring, Maryland, Linstok Press.